BORN POOR; DIE RICH

for

THOU SHALL NOT BE POOR

I0099318

BY

KAYODE ENIRAIYETAN

JESUS FRIENDS MINISTRY PUBLISHING

BORN POOR; DIE RICH *for* THOU SHALL NOT BE POOR

JESUS' FRIENDS MINISTRY

53, Northfleet House,

Tabard Garden Estate ,

London. SE1 1YX.

Tel. & Fax: 02070182426.

Mob.07404736100, 07951775255, 07427942000.

e-mail: jesusfriends28@yahoo.com

Website: www.jesusfriendsministry.com

Text C KayodeEniraiyetan 2016

ISBN: 978-0-9563295-5-4

Books by same author – **Affliction- Fruit of Sin.**

The Redeemed Man.

King David's Twelve Steps To Success.

7 Walls Surrounding A Born Again Christian.

Direct copyright enquires to; **Jesus' Friends Ministry.**

Unless otherwise stated, all scripture quotations are taken from;

The Holy Bible – King James Version, Dake's Annotated Reference Bible,

Bible Basics (Discovering Truth Series),

The Oxford Companion to the Bible – Mtzger&Coogan.

DEDICATION

Dedicated to my family, friends and acquaintances who desire to embark on the journey of success through the path of righteousness and holiness.

<u>CONTENTS</u>

PREFACE

Life is like a square based pyramid where the journey of success is the task to reach the peak of the pyramid.

Each side has different features and hence different means needed for the journey to the top of the pyramid.

Some come to this world on the side with easy access to the peak of the pyramid. To them, there is a natural lift which they only need to press the button and they are lifted up to the peak of the life's pyramid. These are those that are born with the "Golden Spoon" in their mouth. Another side comes with natural steps like a ladder. Each step takes those on this side nearer to the peak. There are lessons to be learnt at each stage and step with its associated ups and downs. Naturally each step must be taken one at a time.

Some are born to the side whose sloppy feature makes it look like a cliff. Here you need a rope to get to the top. But believe me, there is always an invisible rope. We call it a miracle when used. Another side is very slippery. This side is covered with snow that had been turned to ice. Unless you follow a mentor who create steps on the ice along the way, for you to step on, getting to the top will be a mirage.

There are common features to all travellers on this journey of success. Nobody is born blank. We all come to this world equipped with tools needed for each to build his or her Temple of Success. Different as they are, these are talents given to us by our creator. We do not determine them, but we are to discover them. The earlier we discover them, the easier for us to fulfil our purpose in life and the earlier we construct our Temple of Success.

The author's aim in writing this book is to create awareness in you that when you were born into this world, you were endowed with certain inborn traits, the result of millions of years of evolutionary changes and heredity of thousand ancestors. Added to these inborn traits, you acquire many other qualities according to the nature of your environment and the teaching you received during your early childhood. Application of these endowments together with the added qualities will take you to the promised land.

You are therefore the sum total of that which was born in you and that which you have picked up from your experiences, what you have thought and what you have been taught since birth. Application of the above in you, together with your desire to be successful is all what you need to reach your goal, irrespective of how, where and when you are born, all things being equal.

You are therefore the architect of your Temple of Success and your tools to construct this temple are your Thoughts and Actions.

Success is not attainable single-handedly. Various studies of successful people in whatever field had revealed that the desire to be successful must be accompanied by harmonious relationship between two or more people toward the same goal. It must also be a goal that will be mutually beneficial to all concerned in the transaction. Mutual efforts are the key to success.

Success involves obtaining knowledge, applying the knowledge obtained constructively and for the benefit of mankind, you then become magnet for success from the remuneration that such will bring. Nobody is an island.

Genius		CREATES		ideas.
The	wise	DEVELOPS	the	ideas.
The	prudent	APPLIES	the	ideas.
Using	ordinary	to EXECUTE	the	ideas.

We need each other and the journey of success is not the one to embark alone.

Your talent or skill, your level of education or your nationality notwithstanding, without the right attitude; all efforts to a successful life are efforts in futility. A bad attitude is like a flat tyre of a car, it cannot move forward properly unless changed.

I MYSELF DO NOTHING. THE HOLY SPIRIT ACCOMPLISHED ALL THROUGH ME.

ACKNOWLEDGEMENT

Acknowledgement solely to GOD the FATHER, GOD the SON and GOD the HOLY GHOST who are the providers of all the ingredients for this book.

BORN POOR; DIE RICH

for

THOU SHALL NOT BE POOR

CHAPTER ONE

Poverty Defined

The word poor is defined as having little or no money, goods or other means of support. It further means to depend upon charity or public support.

A poor person will lack enough food, clothing, education or healthcare. Such person lives in areas that are prone to diseases, crime and natural disasters. Their basic civil and human rights are often non-existent.

Poverty is synonymous with lack or scarcity, for to be poor in something is to lack that particular thing.

TYPES:

There are three types of poverty;

    1. **MATERIAL POVERTY**

    2. **SPIRITUAL POVERTY** and

    3. **INTELLECTUAL POVERTY**.

We will be confined only to Material Poverty for the sake of this discussion with little references to Spiritual Poverty.

Material Poverty is scarcity, dearth or the state of one who lacks a certain amount of material possessions or money. Absolute Poverty or destitution refers to the deprivation of basic human needs which includes food, water, sanitation, clothing, shelter, health care and education.

THIS CAN BECOME FRICTION FOR ABILLITY TO CREATE WEALTH.

Relative poverty is defined as economic inequality in the location or society in which people live.

In Deuteronomy 15 verse 4, Moses, while addressing the Israelites, informed them of when there will be no poor people among them – 'Save when there shall be no poor among you; for the Lord shall greatly bless thee in the land which the Lord thy God gives thee for an inheritance to possess it' i.e. To the end that there be no poor among you.

It has been anticipated that, given the blessing God will bless the Israelites in the land given for them to possess, a time shall come when poverty would had been eradicated among them (all things being equal).

The basic prescription to escape the unfortunate menace of poverty is to put in place strategies for increasing income to make basic needs more affordable.

Wealth creation is the best way to eliminate poverty and the degree or level of the ability to create the wealth will determine level of wealth acquired or accumulated, all things being equal.

A slack hand becomes poor but the hand of the diligent make rich.

Some poverties are naturally endowed while some are self-impoverishment. Naturally-endowed poverty for an example is when one is born or raised in poor environment. **THIS AGAIN CAN CREATE CONSTRAINT FOR ABILLITY TO CREATE WEALTH.**

Self-impoverishment is where individual decides not to pursue means of wealth creation. Or in the case of a nation, it can be as a result of bad leadership and corruption. It could also be as a result of lack of natural resources.

Poverty, being unfortunate as it is, can be avoided except poverty caused by natural or circumstantial disaster. Thus it can be eliminated or reduced. It can be avoided if those going through it so desire to get out of it.

In the olden days, protection and special care for these economically deprived members of society was the responsibility of Kings who demonstrated their power in part by their ability to help those unable to help themselves. What was incumbent on the Kings or leaders of society as a whole was also required of the individuals. Thus this ethical obligation was continually stressed in the Scripture where those who oppressed the poor were called the wicked and those who help the poor were to be rewarded or blessed. God Himself has His own duty of Providence towards His creations. (See 'The Redeemed Man' – Doctrine of Providence) God's compassion to the poor was so intense such that He considers it as lending to Him if you have pity upon the poor.

Spiritual poverty is a state of being spiritual destitute, a spiritual emptiness. Jesus was speaking of being spiritually poor when He said 'Blessed are the poor in spirit for theirs is the kingdom of God'. This is to recognise your utter spiritual bankruptcy before God.

It is understanding that you have absolutely nothing of worth to offer God. A complete surrender all to God.

Being poor in spirit is admitting that because of your sin, you are completely destitute spiritually and can do nothing to deliver yourself from your dire situation. What Jesus is saying is that; no matter your status in life, you must recognise your spiritual poverty before you can come to God in faith to receive the salvation He offers. So when Jesus says 'Blessed are the poor in spirit, for theirs is the kingdom of heaven', He is declaring that, before we can enter God's kingdom, we must recognise the utter worthlessness of our own spiritual currency and the inability of our own works to save us. REMEMBER; SALVATION IS BY GRACE THROUGH FAITH, NOT OF WORK (Eph.2 8-9)

CHAPTER TWO

THOU SHALL NOT BE POOR

Poor people have managed to overcome some of these handicaps through their resilience and resourcefulness, often helped by their spirituality and love of family. Until the 18th century, poverty was seen as inevitable. But since the 1880s the reduction in extreme poverty – from three-quarters to one-fifth of the world's population- shows that the number of poor people in the world can be further reduced, if not eliminated.

It is very unfortunate that so many people are falling into poverty at a time when it's almost illegal to be poor. That is why it amount to offence against humanity when an able body starts to engaged in any of the biological necessities of life like sitting, sleeping, lying down or loitering and not engage in any wealth creating activities. Your heart will always be where your treasure is: so if your treasure is to be unproductive, your mind will pursue unproductive activities, but if it is towards wealth creation, your engagement will surely be directed towards wealth creating activities.

The Israelites were told 'Save when there shall be no poor among you ----- because he knew that it is possible for poverty to be completely eliminated if some conditions are met. As mentioned earlier; the prescription to escape being poor is to ensure you generate more income than expenses. Therefore, we need to believe that; **WE ARE NOT MEANT TO BE POOR**.

In fact, it is inexcusable to be poor – given the ample resources God bestowed on mankind and the various talents given to man to extract those resources.

IF GOD SAYS HE IS GOING TO BLESS YOU IF YOU DO SOMETHING, IT IS YOUR CHOICE IF YOU LOOSE THAT BLESSING BECAUSE OF YOUR DISOBEDIENCE. GOD WILL ALWAYS KEEP HIS PROMISE.

The blessing is not free; it comes on the condition that man hearkens into the voice of the Lord and observes to do His commandments. The emphasis to obey God and observe His commandments and be blessed with a prosperous life and good success was also made to mankind --- for then thou shalt make thy way prosperous and then thou shalt have good success.

It therefore comes to the fact that;

YOU ARE NOT DESTINED TO DIE POOR EVEN WHEN BORN POOR.

I congratulate and rejoice with every person who is experiencing every thought, every feeling and every hardship that come to those who travel that road. I believe in poverty as a condition to experience, to go through, and then to get out of. It is not a condition to stay in.

People may say how do you get out of poverty? No one can definitely tell another that. No two persons can find the same way out. Each must find his own way out himself and that depends on him. The first step is to desire a purpose. The purpose must then be backed up with effort and willingness to work. This mean willingness to work at anything that comes your way, no matter what, so long as it means "the way out of poverty". Not pick and choose but what comes and doing it the best way you know how. It means doing the work well while still doing it even when you do not like it and not longer than necessary. You have to use every rung in the ladder as a rung to the one above.

It meant effort, but out of the effort and the work comes the experience; the up building the development, the capacity to understand and sympathize, the greatest heritage that can come to a man. And nothing in the world can give that to a man so that it will burn into him, as will poverty. I repeat; always a condition to work out of, not to stay in.

MAY YOUR WAY TO SUCCESS BE ROUGH; OR HOW DO YOU GAIN THE EXPERIENCE TO SUSTAIN IT WHEN IT FINALLY COMES?

REQUIREMENTS TO ESCAPE THE MENANCE OF POVERTY.

There are three basic requirements needed for man/woman to live a prosperous life and have good success;

1. **BELIEVE IN GOD AND FEAR HIM**.

2. **MAINTAIN A GOOD HEALTH**.

3. **DEVELOP A SKILL**.

BELIEVE IN GOD AND FEAR HIM. – The fear of the Lord is the beginning of wisdom. It is interesting to note that this principle is the first word of wisdom in the Book of Proverb. It is therefore not a coincidence that the wisest man on earth King Solomon made it the first word of wisdom in the book of the wise.

Nothing is too difficult for our creator to do. In fact, He asked us; 'Is anything too difficult for me to do? He brought out drinking water from rock in the wilderness for His people to drink, He paid tax from the mouth of a fish creating the first ATM, We witnessed the first submarine when Jonah stayed in the belly of a fish for three days. Nothing is too difficult for God to do. It is for us to ask and we shall be given, to seek and we shall find and to knock for doors to open for us.

He expects us to: 1. Trust Him to provide for us.

 2. Obey His commandment and do what He tells us to do.

 3. Believe that God will do it.

There is no financial crisis in God's kingdom! When the Israelites hungered and thirsted; He sent them fresh manna, and provided water from the rock. He assigned ravens to feed Elijah. He multiplied oil and flour to sustain a destitute widow's family. He fed thousands from a boy's lunch of five loaves and two fishes.

He promised that the lamb will provide you with cloth, and the goats with the price of a field. This in effect means that you will have plenty to feed you and your family when you sell the goats and you will be clothed by the wool from the lamb. God will provide all your needs according to His riches in glory. These are without limit I tell you.

MAINTAIN A GOOD HEALTH. –Apart from some natural or unfortunate calamity, you were born perfect and with good health and this should be maintained along the line while growing up. Most of us through what we eat or drink damage our health all in the process of having a nice time. Accident can happen I know, but most of times self-destruction account for most of our ill-health.

A person of good health is already one of the wealthiest people in the world. Such a person already has all he/she needs to make it to the top of the mountain.

Let us face it; what is the worth of the following:- 1. Your good health. 2. To live in a good environment or peaceful country, what has it cost you in pounds? 3. What is your freedom worth in monetary term? 4. Your eyes? Would you rather exchange your eyes for a million pounds? 5. How about your hands and feet? Are they worth £100,000,000.00? 6. That bright mind and your intelligence, what is its worth to you? Remember the saying; **HEALTH IS WEALTH**.

Best Doctors in the world;

 - **DOCTOR DIET,**

- **DOCTOR QUIET &**

- **DOCTOR MERRYMAN.**

DEVELOP A SKILL:- Each one of us is a miracle; all of us to some degree indulge in some dreams and wishes; part of which is to be free from wants, to live in a fine house, to drive fine car, to wear designer clothes, eat good food, send our children to best schools etc. Why not, since we live in a land of unlimited opportunities.

We fail to achieve the above because majority of us have absolutely no idea how to make our dreams come true. Each individual is blessed with a specific talent or tools necessary to create a magnificent life, but we do not realise our talents or how to use them rightly. What good are these talents when you do not realise that you have them or do not know how to use them.

Even when your skill or talent is natural, there is need for you to develop and uphold such skill in order to maintain it. Developing your skill begins with assessing which skills are important for your desired career development.

Everyone wants to have a fulfilling career. To achieve this, you need to follow your heart and you need to live to your fullest potential. Your deep satisfaction will come when you know you have done your best. The key to living your fullest potential is developing your skill so that you can get better and better over time.

Your skill development should follow the 70-20-10 rule:

70% of your development should come from on-the job activities and action learning. This can include development experiences like managing a project, serving on a cross-functional team, taking on a new task, job shadowing, and job rotation.

20% of your development should come from interactions with others. This includes having a mentor, being a mentor, coaching, participating in communities of practice and serving as a leader in a staff organisation.

10% of your development should come from training, including classes, seminars, webinars and conferences.

Once you have identified the skills you need to develop to achieve your career goals, your next step is identifying how you will develop your skills.

The two main avenues for developing your skills are through the following; 1. Education and Training, and 2. Developmental Experiences.

Here are some tips for developing your skills;

1. **Seek Information**; By seeking information, you know more and your skill become more fun and enjoyable. You will know further and deeper than your colleagues.

2. **Be open to learning**; Be motivated. An essential ingredient to have good learning

skill is motivation. If you are motivated to learn about a subject, it will be much easier to learn it.

3. **Be a Versatilist**; A versatilist is someone who can easily adapt to new situations and quickly develop the skills necessary to excel. Being a versatilist means being a smart learner who knows what to learn and how to quickly learn it. A versatilist should anticipate the future. That way he will get a sense of what new skills will be in demand and prepare himself before most people do.

4. **Find a Role Model**; It will be easier for you to grow if you have living examples of what you want to be. Your role model gives you a standard to achieve so that you know where and how far you should go in developing your skills. It will also motivate you since you know that someone has already achieved such high standard.

5. **Find a Mentor**; Developing your skill will be much more easier if you work with

those who have gone through it. That's why one should find not just role models but also mentors. Ideally your mentor is also your role model but at least they are those who are more experienced than you. In the field. These people can teach you what to do and what not to do so that you don't have to find them yourself the hard way. This can save you a lot of time. Finding a mentor is not easy and sometimes you may have to give or make sacrifice before someone become your mentor. Try to be useful to them and try to give them reasons to invest their time in you.

6. **Undertake Real Project**; The best way to develop your skills is through real projects. Real project gives you the experience upon which your development will be based. Do not wait until everything is well prepared before working on real project. You will face failures in the process but they are your stepping stones to success since they give you precious lessons.

7. **Build on Your Success**; Have feedback on the real projects you had undertaken.

Correct mistakes and your weaknesses and build on your success. Continue on the path that lead to success and improve on them.

CHAPTER THREE

SUCCESS

One of the most common mistakes and one of the costliest is thinking that success is due to some genius, some magic, something or other which we do not possess.

Success is: - **Knowing your purpose in life**

Growing to reach your maximum potential

Sowing seeds that benefit others.

Not to be poor is to be economically independent or secured. Your economic security does not lie in your job alone; it lies in your own power to **PRODUCE**, to **THINK**, to **LEAN**, to **CREATE** or to **ADOPT**.

These are true Financial Independence. It is not having **WEALTH**, it is having the **POWER**, the **SKILL** to produce wealth. As mentioned earlier, the prescription against poverty is to put in place strategies for income creation enough to meet your basic needs.

I use the word "develop" deliberately because having a skill is not enough. Your skill, whether acquired or natural need to be developed and nurtured towards reaching its maximum potential. Success is a journey and not a destination. Your success attained today need to be developed towards your maximum capability.

Your success in life or otherwise depends on you and nothing else. Your heart will always be where your treasure is and if your treasure is to be unproductive, your mind will pursue unproductive activities, but if it is towards wealth creation, your engagement in life will surely be directed towards wealth creating activities.

The desire to be successful and make it in life must originate from you and from this will arouse your propensity to succeed in life. Remember the saying; **your destiny is in your hand.**

Our lives naturally break into two halves, with a midpoint usually falling somewhere between ages thirty and fifty.

The first half of life has to do with getting, gaining, learning and earning. The second half is more risky because it has to do with living beyond the immediate.

You need to take responsibility and order your life so that your second half is better than the first or else you will join the ranks of those who are coasting their way to retirement.

You need to make your second half count and be significant such that you will experience a life of purpose and see the fulfilment of your life's mission. As you make progress on the success journey, you will frequently find yourself standing at crossroads when you'll have to make decision. You will have to gain something, lose something or trade something.

In the early life, those decisions will either make you add or subtract value to your life, but as time goes by it gets more complicated and if you want to keep going forward, you usually have to make more trade – offs.

At the crossroad, if you hope for situation where you can receive without giving anything up, you will loses because it rarely comes. **YOU HAVE TO GIVE UP TO GO UP**. And the people who want to move forward without making any sacrifices get stuck at the crossroads and never go any further on the success journey. **THERE IS NO SUCCESS WITHOUT SACRIFICE**.

In the trade – offs, there must be willingness to make sacrifices. If you are currently succeeding and you haven't made any sacrifices, then someone who has gone before you has made some that you are benefiting. And if you are making sacrifices now and you are not seeing any success, be assured, either you or someone else will enjoy the fruit of those sacrifices latter on.

The second secret to good trade – off is old-fashioned persistence. Persistence and determination will surely see you through.

When you desire to be successful or dream of success, this shall determine your goals which will map out your course of actions. Your actions create results and results bring you **success**.

The unfortunate thing that I discovered is that many people's mind had been conditioned and enslaved to the notion that they will never make it in life or be successful. They are beaten from the start that they will never amount to much in life. They will always have to stay in the same old rut. They are like the huge circus elephants. They are tied by a chain to small stakes in the ground. They could easily rip off those stakes from the earth and be free but they would not because their minds have been conditioned to stay where they are tied. So also are the minds that believe success is only for the lucky fortunate set of people. You can be what you want to be if you set your mind to it. **AS A MAN THINKS IN HIS HEART SO IS HE.**

It is a well-established fact that a person's acts are always in harmony with the dominating thoughts of his or her mind.

It is very unfortunate that 95% of people of the world are drifting aimlessly through life. **LIVE AIMLESSLY AND YOU BECOME A FAILURE.**

Inaction leads to ATROPHY which leads to loss of ambition and self-confidence.

You will get nowhere if you start nowhere. Let's face it, those who remain in poverty or in perpetual want seldom realise that they are where they are as the result of their own act or inaction.

Since our main business in life is to succeed and a successful living is a journey towards simplicity and a triumph over confusion; we must start that journey of success from when we are young even from when we are in our cradle.

Remember what Abraham Lincoln said; "It is not the years in your life that counts, it's the life in your years". **IT IS NOT HOW LONG, BUT HOW WELL**.

Nature compels us all to move through life. We could not remain stationary however much we wished. Every right-thinking individual wants to move through life to develop and improve mentally and physically and be called a SUCCESS and not just a perambulating entity.

Meanwhile, we are all makers of our destinies and our thoughts and our acts are the tools with which we do the making. We act as we think, and as mentioned earlier, our actions create results and results bring us success.

The world will not pay you with what you know but with what you do with what you know.

While what we know might be influenced by some external factors like our environment and our acquired knowledge, education or experience gained, the use of what we know or what we do with it is entirely up to us.

It is the application of our experience gained and knowledge acquired and to what use these are put that will determine our success or otherwise. **THE VALUE OF A THING IS THE APPLICATION OF IT.**

But then we cannot apply the knowledge which we do not possess, we must therefore secure possession of knowledge; we must seek, acquire and develop the knowledge needed for the attainment of our goal. Seek and you shall find, knock and it shall be opened to you, ask and you shall be given.

KNOWLEDGE IS POWER AND YOU CANNOT BE SUCCESSFUL WITHOUT POWER.

The Scripture says '**My people perish for lack of Knowledge**'.

A SUCCESSFUL LIVING IS A JOURNEY TOWARDS SIMPLICITY AND A TRIUMPH OVER CONFUSION.

It is a journey towards attaining better life and avoidance of confusion.

No matter what you do for a living, no matter how old you are, and regardless of where you grew up, we all share something in common – a desire to be successful. To succeed, you need a burning desire.

True success should be defined by you, specific to you and your goals. Your success and happiness depends on what you contributed not what you received and this is linked to one's self esteem.

What success means to one, can be very different to another. Success to some may mean fancy cars and homes. Success to others may mean being a good parent, spouse, or friend. For others it may simply mean to be happy. Or it can be all of the above. You can only become successful if you BELIEVE in yourself that you will succeed.

Your success, happiness – anything you truly want for your life has to begin with unwavering, non-negotiable desire, commitment and persistence. Without it, you cannot withstand and overcome the tests that will be put in your way, to not only see how badly you really want it, but to help you appreciate what you have once you get it. Because it is through the tests, that you discover yourself and your purpose, which is what you were really looking for to begin with.

Life experience has taught some of us that very few things are out of the realm of our control, so 99 per cent of life is what we make of it.

Consciously or subconsciously, we are constantly making choices, so our life is a series of our own decisions. If your life is miserable, look in the mirror. If you consider your life to be successful and happy, also look in the mirror.

You cannot guarantee success, but you can increase the chance of it happening. Opportunity favours the prepared. One thing is certain; the difference between people who fail and those who succeed is that successful people do the things that failures are afraid to tackle.

Dream Big, Big Achievement Starts With Big Dreams.

Your vision dictates your outcome. If your vision is big, your outcome will be big. If your vision is small, your outcome will be small. You dictate the size of your miracle in life.

Everything you achieve in life will require a vision first. If you cannot see it, then you will not get it. You have to learn to think big.

The seventh miracle of Elisha talked of the increase of the widow's oil. Elisha instructed her to round up all containers, jars and pots she could find. He even told her to borrow from neighbours and anywhere she could find them.

She shut the door behind her and started pouring out the oil as she was instructed. She and her son kept pouring until there were no more empty jars or pot anymore. Then the oil stopped. She ran out of vessels before she ran out of oil.

God provided the amount of oil that she had vision for. If she had provided more vessels, the oil would have filled more. The miracle did not dictate the size of the vision, her vision dictated the size of the miracle she got.

Think big. Have a vision that is big. Then you will end up with big success.

Dreams produce Desires, which in turn translates to Decisions. Decisions are driven by Determination and this must be powered by Diligence, which produces Delivery i.e. SUCCESS. When God is fully involved in all of these processes, Good Success is guaranteed.

FACTORS OF SUCCESS: There are factors that are required for the attainment of a successful life. Some of these factors are enumerated below;

- One must know that whatever he does, he is moving forward towards a goal. Aimlessness is the worst enemy of success. As long as one has purpose, he feels that his energy and creative thought are taking him somewhere, and there is satisfaction at the end of it. Success must therefore be personal for it to be meaningful. It must come from within the individual.

- Success does not climb up in a straight line. It has the intrinsic character of what is called Ups and Downs, the batting average. Sometimes, to become a success you need to learn from your failures. Henry Ford said;- "Failure is simply the opportunity to begin again more intelligently.

- The third factor is the price of the success. There is no free success. The joy of success must be counterbalanced by the effort to achieve it.

THE HOTTER THE BATTLE THE SWEETER THE VICTORY.

Success must come with satisfaction to the successor. Satisfactory to one man may stem from amassing of fortune, while to another man it may come from the writing of a poem. Certainly, neither of them can claim success at all if there is no satisfaction in either the fortune or the poem. Success must be enjoyed. It may be won with tears but it must be crowned with laughter.

- The final basic factor of success is spirituality. Consider Joshua 1 verse 8 – This book of the law shall not depart out of thy mouth; but thou shall meditate therein day and night, that thou may observe to do according to all that is written therein; **FOR THEN THOU SHALL MAKE THY WAY PROSPEROUS, AND THEN THOU SHALL HAVE GOOD SUCCESS**.

Fraudulent accumulation of wealth is no success and that is why in Genesis 3:19, God commanded that – in the sweat of thy face shall thou eat bread.

The successful individual must have a conviction that he is in tune with God. He must be convinced that his success is in line with God's purpose or will for his life.

It must come in tune with God's natural law of existence or God's Doctrine of Providence. (See 'The Redeemed Man' by the same author).

CHAPTER FOUR

THE ROAD TO SUCCESS

Happiness, the final object of all human effort, is a state of mind that can be maintained only through the hope of future achievement. Happiness lies always in the future and never in the past.

The happy person is the one who dreams of heights of achievement that are yet unattained; the home you intend to own, the money you intend to earn and place in the bank, the trip you intend to take when you can afford it, the posit in in life you intend to fill when you have prepared yourself, and the preparation itself – these are the things that produce happiness.

There is a lifelong struggle between the motivating forces and desires of the human mind, which takes place between the impulses of right and wrong. It has also been established that no sane person will deliberately follow the path of failure but rather follow the path of success.

Success in life, no matter what one may call success, is very largely a matter of adaptation to environment in such a manner that there is harmony between the individual and his environment. The palace of a King becomes as a hovel of a peasant if harmony does not abound within its walls. Conversely, the hut of a peasant may be made to yield more happiness than that of the mansion of the rich man if harmony obtains in the former and not in the latter.

Each one of us is a miracle; all of us to some degree indulge in some dreams and aspirations - - - to be free from wants, to live in a fine house, to drive fine car, to wear designer's clothes, eat good food, send our children to best schools. We fail to achieve those dreams because majority of us have absolutely no idea how to make our dreams come true.

Each individual is blessed with a specific talent or tools necessary to create a magnificent life, but we do not realise our talent, or when we do we do not know how to use them rightly. Those dreams and aspirations that we had must be manifested in our life and become true before we can claim to achieve success.

A man's chief business in life is to succeed. The road to success may be, and generally is, obstructed by many influences which must be removed before the goal can be reached. One of the most detrimental of these obstacles is that of unfortunate alliance with minds which do not harmonize. In such cases the alliance must be broken or the end is sure to be defeat and failure.

Man experience is acquired through two forms of heredity. Physical heredity and Social heredity.

Through the law of Physical heredity, man has slowly evolved from the amoeba (a single-cell animal form), through stages of development corresponding to all the known animal forms now on this earth, including those which are known to have existed but which are now extinct.

Every generation through which man has passed has added to his nature something of the traits, habits and physical appearances of that generation.

Man physical inheritance therefore, is a heterogeneous collection of many habits and physical forms.

By far the most important part of man's make-up comes to him through the law of social heredity. This term having reference to the methods by which one generation imposes upon the minds of the generation under its immediate control the superstitions, belief, legends and ideas which it, in turn, inherited from the generation preceding.

Social heredity mean any and all sources through which a person acquires knowledge, such as schooling of religious and all other natures; reading, word of mouth conversation, story-telling and all manner of thought inspiration coming from what is generally accepted as one's "personal experience".

Thus through the operation of the law of social heredity, anyone having control of the mind of a child may, through intense teaching, plant in that child's mind any idea, whether false or true, in such a manner that the child accepts it as true and it becomes as much a part of the child's personality as any cell or organ of its physical body and just as hard to change in its nature.

It is through the law of social heredity that the religionist plants in the child's mind dogmas and creeds and religious ceremonies too numerous to describe, holding those ideas before that mind until the mind accepts them and forever seals them as a part of its irrevocable belief.

The mind of a child which has not come into the age of general understanding, during an average period covering let us say, the first two years of its life, is plastic, open, clean and free. Any idea planted in such a mind by one in whom the child has confidence takes root and grows, so to speak, in such a manner that it never can be eradicated or wiped out, no matter how opposed to logic or reason that idea may be.

Many religionist claim that they can so deeply implant the tenets of their religion in the mind of a child that there never can be room in that mind for any other religion, either in whole or in part.

In the same manner, if we can implant the desire to be a success through the path of righteousness in the mind of the child, it will take root and grow to such extent that it never can be eradicated or wiped out. The child will follow the path of success and not of failure. In fact, there will be no room for failure in the mind of the child.

Man has been endowed with the power to use the most highly organised form of energy known to man, that of thought. It is not improbable that thought is the closest connecting link there is between the material, physical things of this world and the world of Divinity. You have not only the power to think, you have the power to control your thoughts and direct them to do your bidding. You have within your control the power to select the material that constitute the dominating thoughts of your mind. Those thoughts which dominate your mind will bring you success or failure according to their nature.

It has been said earlier that without power there can be no success. The magic key that will unlock the door to the source of power is your thought and you may make use of it the moment you learn to control your thought. The point I wish clearly to establish here is that thought, whether accurate or inaccurate, is the most highly organized functioning power of your mind; and that you are the sum total of your dominating or most prominent thoughts.

Another way man acquires knowledge and or experience is through man's environment.

We absorb the material for thought from our surrounding environment where this environment consists of books we read, the people with whom we associate, the community in which we live, the nature of the work in which we are engaged, the country or nation in which we reside, the songs we are accustomed to, and most important of all, the religion and intellectual training we receive prior to the age of fourteen years.

The mind and invariably our thought feed upon that which we supply it, or that which is forced upon it, through our environment. Therefore we need to select the environment that will supply the mind with suitable materials out of which to carry on its work of attaining goal that lead to success and not failure.

We therefore need to select our environment, as far as possible, with the object of supplying the mind with suitable material out of which to carry on its work of attaining our goal. If your environment is not to your liking, change it.

The first step is to create in your own mind an exact, clear and well-rounded out picture of the environment in which you believe you could best attain your chief goal and then concentrate your mind upon this picture until you transform it into reality. The first principle to be observed in your plans for the achievement of success is to create in your mind a clear, well defined picture of that which you intend to accomplish. If you fail or neglect to observe it, you cannot succeed, except by chance.

Your daily associates constitute one of the most important and influential parts of your environment, and may work for your progress or your retrogression, according to the nature of those associates. As far as possible, you should select as your most intimate daily associates, those who are in sympathy with your aims and ideas, especially those represented by your goal and whose mental attitude inspires you with enthusiasm, self-confidence, determination and ambition.

Every word spoken within our hearing, every sight that reaches our eyes, every sense impression that we receive through any of the five senses, influences our thoughts.

Every man is the reflection of the thought he has entertained during his lifetime. That is; you are as you think.

Success is a journey, not a destination, and that journey must start from when we are still in the cradle.

Man also is the architect of his own 'Temple of Success' and the tools with which he builds that temple is his thoughts and his actions.

As these thoughts are being influenced by experiences gathered by hereditary and environmental factors, as earlier explained, individual, destined for success must start to plant that seed of success right from when he was at the period of infancy (the first seven years of his life) and watered by knowledge and skill gathered or acquired from hereditary and environmental factors. Lack of these knowledge, skill and experience can only result in one thing 'FAILURE'. My people perish because of lack of knowledge says the Scripture I repeat.

After being equipped with the above knowledge experiences a person wishing to continue on the path to succeed must 1. Have a definite goal and 2. Must be ready to back that definite goal with burning desire to achieve the definite goal.

A burning desire for a goal will lead to the appropriate action through which the goal will manifest. From the time that you plant a definite purpose in your mind, your mind begins, both consciously and unconsciously, to gather and store away the material with which you are to accomplish that purpose.

Desire is the factor which determines what your definite purpose in life shall be. No one can select your dominating desire for you, but once you select it yourself it becomes your definite chief goal and occupies the spotlight of your mind until it is satisfied by transformation into reality, unless you permit it to be pushed aside by conflicting desires.

A definite goal purpose is something that you must create for yourself. No one else will create it for you and it will not create itself.

Start now to analyse your desires and find out what it is that you wish, and then make up your mind to get it. You are a contractor and builder, and like men who build house out of mere wood and brick and steel, you must draw up a set of plans after which to shape your success building. **YOU GO NOWHERE IF YOU START NOWHERE**.

Your first step is to decide what your major aim in life shall be. Your next step is statement in writing of the plan or plans through which you intend to attain the object of your aim. Your next step will be the forming of an alliance with some person or persons who will cooperate with you in carrying out these plans and transforming your definite chief aim into reality.

The alliance should be made between yourself and those who have your highest and best interests at heart.

If you are a married man your wife should be one of the members of this alliance, providing there exists between you a normal state of confidence and sympathy. Other members of this alliance may be your mother, father, brothers or sisters or some close friend friends.

If you are a single person your sweetheart, if you have one, should become a member of your alliance. This is a result of studying one of the most powerful laws of the human mind.

You will then have to support this goal with sufficient self-confidence. Without self-confidence, it will be very difficult to progress to the next stage which is one of the most important step on your road to success; to take initiative to act and transform your goal to reality.

The workshop in which the above can be brought together into reality is the process of imagination. The selection of definite Chief goal calls for the use of both imagination and decision. Meanwhile the power of decision grows with use.

It is a well-known fact that the only manner in which an over pampered boy or girl may be made to become useful is by forcing him or her to become self-sustaining. This calls for the exercise of both imagination and decision, neither of which would be used except out of necessity.

CHAPTER FIVE

STAGES OF LIFE

Since we have established that our journey of success must start from when we are young, we therefore must examine various stages of the journey and what happens at each stage.

Man's life span is divided into three stages of life called THE STAGES OF LIFE.

The movement through the stages is a progression. As we pass from one stage to the next, often with some difficult periods of transition, we learn and mature in the process.

As important as the stages themselves are, changes periods between stages are the periods of most obvious significant. They are times which are sometimes difficult, but preparation and understanding do help. If we acknowledge and work through the issue of each successive stage, we become better human and spiritual beings.

The ages shown for each stage are only rough estimates. People may pass through the stages several years earlier or later than the estimates shown.

Individuals vary widely in their progression through the stages.

Ages 1 to 30; This is the Morning stage and also called SUNRISE AGE. It is the rising stage of life which is the developmental stage. It is the age of Getting, Learning and Earning. The age of Vitality, Playfulness, Imaginations, Ingenuity and Passion. This stage embodies the principle of Innovation and Transformation. This is the age that the young is taught, by all methods, any idea, dogma, creed, religion or system of ethical conduct by its parents or those who may have authority over it, before reaching the age at which it may reason and reflect upon such teaching in its own way; estimating such reaching power at ages seven to twelve years.

Start with dependent stage particularly between one to three years. It involves brain development, learning motor skills and sensory abilities. Growing and mastering motor skills and languages. Learning to play and socialize. Continued growth, formal school and organized activities. From 10-19 years, puberty brings hormonal changes and reactions including behavioural risks. Towards the end of these period features completing education and beginning of career and family. Potential coping and financial pressures starts from here.

Ages 31 to 49 -This is the Afternoon stage also called SUNSHINE AGE. This is the age where we practice what we had been learning in the previous Morning Stage of life. The sun is now shinning on what had been previously learnt or gathered. It is the fruitful age. It is also the Age of Abnormality. Abnormality because you work more than normal. In the previous stage of life, you can afford to work or gather knowledge at the normal speed, but here, you have to do all what you need more so as to have good rest in the coming span of life. Age of Enterprising and the need to go out into the world and make our mark. It is the Midlife stage when we take deeper meaning of our lives for better to forge ahead with new understandings.

Adult life indeed. This also includes the Middle Age. Here you manage family and career growth. Most couples start families in this stage. Continued coping with pressures.

Ages 50 Upward - This is the Evening Stage also called SUNSET AGE. It is the resting stage as we need rest after working hard. God also rested. At this span of life, we are getting ready to sleep and go to meet our maker. It is the Age where truth about God and godliness must finally done on us. It is the Age of reality. For example; any individual at this stage that have just started to compile his/her Curriculum Vitae for the purpose of looking for work must have missed it. Mature Adulthood when we have raised families established ourselves in our work life and become contributors to the betterment of society through volunteerism, mentorships and other forms of philanthropy. Age of Benevolence. Age of wisdom when we have acquired a rich repository of experiences that can be used to guide others while we reap the benefits of life's lessons.

First signs of ageing and effects of lifestyle; menopause, children are leaving the nest, grandchildren arrive, career peak. Ageing parent may require care.

From age 60 upward, there will be more signs of ageing and lifestyle effects. May start to enjoy Government's benefits provided retirement and health care or private pensions. Retirement discretionary time. Some health problems and medications. May care for others.

By Age 70; one becomes vulnerable elder. It is the beginning of frailty, cognitive or multiple health problems and medications. Some may require assistance. Not able to drive. Possible move to Assisted living. By Age 80; one becomes Dependent elder. Requires daily care. Unable to perform all personal functions. Possible move to a nursing home.

CAREER PLANNING

We are born helpless. We can't walk, can't talk, can't feed ourselves can't even do our own cleaning.

As children, the way we're wired to learn is by watching and mimicking others. First we learn to do physical skills like walk and talk. Then we develop social skills by watching and mimicking our peers around us. Then, finally, in late childhood, we learn to adapt to our culture by observing the rules and norms around us and trying to behave in such a way that is generally considered acceptable by society.

In this stage, we are typically developing personal autonomy and leaving the family to establish an independent home, finances and so on. We are developing our own sense of personhood as separate from parents and childhood peer groups. We try our new relationships such as romantic interests, professional associates, peer groups and friends. This is typical a period of tentative or provisional commitments. We are comfortable there is plenty of time ahead to change our minds on provisional decisions concerning things like location, occupation, plans to marry or not to marry, friends, key life values and so on. Our focus is on defining ourselves as individuals and establishing an initial life structure.

The goal of this Sunrise Stage is to teach us how to function within society so that we can be autonomous, self-sufficient adults. The idea is that the adults in the community around us help us to reach this point through supporting our ability to make decisions and take action ourselves. But some adults and community members around us are defiant. They punish us for our independence. They don't support our decisions. And therefore we don't develop autonomy. We get stuck in the early stage, endlessly mimicking those around us, endlessly attempting to please all so that we might not be judged.

This is usually a period of significant turmoil – of looking at who we are becoming and asking if we are really journeying in directions we want to go. We question most of our earlier tentative choices. Have we made the right decisions? Are we running out of time for changing our decisions? Are our decisions becoming permanent before we want them to? Do we really want to make this location, career path or romantic relationship permanent? Will we or will we not settle down and have a family? Is time running out? Often with considerable angst similar to the better known mid-life crisis, we rethink our provisional decisions and maintain them or change them in the process of making more permanent choices.

In a "normal" healthy individual, Sunrise Stage will last until late adolescence and early adulthood. For some people, it may last further into adulthood. A select few wake up one day at age 45 realizing they've never actually lived for themselves and wonder where the hell the years went. The constant search for approval and validation. The absence of independent thought and personal values must be replaced and we must develop the ability to act by ourselves and for ourselves.

SUNSHINE STAGE: SELF-DISCOVERY

In Sunrise stage, we learn to fit in with the people and culture around us. Sunshine Stage is about learning *what makes us different* from the people and culture around us. This Stage requires us to begin making decisions for ourselves, to test ourselves, and to understand ourselves and what makes us unique.

This is typically a period of relative order and stability where we implement and live the choices made in the young adult transition. We settle down into deeper commitments involving work, family, church, and our communities' ties and so on. We focus on accomplishment, becoming our own persons and generating an inner sense of expertise and mastery of our professions. By now we have a better developed and fairly well defined, though not usually final, dream of what we want to achieve in life. We put significant energy into achieving the dream.

The Sunshine Stage involves a lot of trial-and-error and experimentation. We experiment with living in new places, hanging out with new people, imbibing new substances, and playing with new people's orifices. The Stage is a process of self-discovery. We try things. Some of them go well. Some of them don't. The goal is to stick with the ones that go well and move on.

Here we tend to question everything again. If we have not achieved our dreams we wonder why not. Were they really the right dreams? If we have achieved our dreams we look at what values we might have neglected in their pursuit. Was it worth it? Either way we are probably disillusioned. A period of reassessment and realignment usually takes place, including recognition and re-balancing of key polarities.

So we're just bad at some things. Then there are other things that are great for a while, but begin to have diminishing returns after a few years. Your limitations are important because you must eventually come to the realization that your time on this planet is limited and you should therefore spend it on things that matter most. That means realizing that just because you *can* do something, doesn't mean you should do it. That means realizing that just because you like certain people doesn't mean you should be with them. That means realizing that there are opportunity costs to everything and that <u>you can't have it all</u>.

There are some people who never allow themselves to feel limitations — either because they refuse to admit their failures, or because they delude themselves into believing that their limitations don't exist. These people get stuck in Sunshine Stage.

These are the "serial entrepreneurs" who are 38 and living with mom and still haven't made any money after 15 years of trying. These are the "aspiring actors" who are still waiting tables and haven't done an audition in two years. These are the people who can't settle into a long-term relationship because they always have a gnawing feeling that there's someone better around the corner. These are the people who brush all of their failings aside as "releasing" negativity into the universe or "purging" their baggage from their lives.

At some point we all must admit the inevitable: life is short, not all of our dreams can come true, and so we should carefully pick and choose what we have the best shot at and commit to it. Some experts stress that acknowledging the turmoil, experiencing the pain, and facing and resolving the polarities is essential for continued growth and satisfaction. Refusing to acknowledge or experience the mid-life anxieties and question or at some unconscious level trying to go back and be twenty again is usually a sure way to get stuck and disgruntled in a way station.

SUNSET STAGE: LEAVING LEGACY AND COMMITMENT

The period after completion of the mid-life transition can be one of the most productive of all stages. Once you've pushed your own boundaries and either found your limitations (i.e., athletics, the culinary arts) or found the diminishing returns of certain activities (i.e., partying, video games) then you are left with what are both (a) actually important to you, and (b) what you're not terrible at. Now it's time to make your dent in the world. We are usually at the peak of our mature abilities here. If the issues of the mid-life transition have been acknowledged and addressed we can make our greatest possible contribution to others and society.

Sunset Stage is the great consolidation of one's life. Out go the friends who are and holding you back. Out go the activities and hobbies that are a mindless waste of time. Here we can be less driven, less ego-centred, less compelled to compete with and impress others. Instead we can focus on what really matters to us, on developing younger people, on community with others, on leaving some personal legacy that really makes things better for people (whether it is recognised as our personal legacy or not), and on accomplishing values that our maturity and greater spirituality tell us have the most true meaning in the overall scheme of life.

Then you double down on what you're best at and what is best to you. You double down on the most important relationships in your life. You double down on a single mission in life, whether that's to work on the world's energy crisis or to be a bitching digital artist or to become an expert in brains or have a bunch of snotty, drooling children. Whatever it is, Sunset Stage is when you get it done.

Sunset Stage is all about maximizing your own potential in this life. It's all about building your legacy. What will you leave behind when you're gone? What will people remember you by? Whether that's a breakthrough study or an amazing new product or an adoring family, this Stage is about leaving the world a little bit different than the way you found it.

Sunset Stage ends when a combination of two things happens: 1) you feel as though there's not much else you are able to accomplish, and 2) you get old and tired and find that you would rather relax and do crossword puzzles all day.

People who get lodged in Sunset Stage often do so because they don't know how to let go of their ambition and constant desire for more. This inability to let go of the power and influence they crave counteracts the natural calming effects of time and they will often remain driven and hungry well into their 70s and 80s.

People arrive into this last Stage having spent somewhere around half a century investing them in what they believed was meaningful and important. They did great things, worked hard, earned everything they have, maybe started a family or a charity or a political or Cultural Revolution or two, and now they're done. They've reached the age where their energy and circumstances no longer allow them to pursue their purpose any further.

The goal of the last Stage then becomes not to create a legacy as much as simply making sure that legacy lasts beyond one's death. This is the stage of tying things up, of completing the design of what we want to become, of finalizing our growth and assessing or fine-tuning the person we have made of ourselves.

This could be something as simple as supporting and advising their (now grown) children and living vicariously through them. It could mean passing on their projects and work to a protégé or apprentice. It could also mean becoming more politically active to maintain their values in a society that they no longer recognize.

The last Stage is important psychologically because it makes the ever-growing reality of one's own mortality more bearable. As humans, we have a deep need to feel as though our lives mean something. This meaning we constantly search for is literally our only psychological defence against the incomprehensibility of this life and the inevitability of our own death. To lose that meaning, or to watch it slip away, or to slowly feel as though the world has left you behind, is to stare oblivion in the face and let it consume you willingly.

This stage can go on for many years. It can be hopeful or cynical depending on how realistically, humbly, and effectively we have resolved or now finally resolved the issues faced in earlier stages. We may move into this stage sooner or later depending on how rapidly we have developed in earlier stages – how much we have moved beyond our narrow selves. Here we come to grips with the ultimate limitations of life, ourselves and morality. We can look hopefully and unflinchingly at the ultimate meaning of our life and the life of others in the larger context. We do the best we can to pass whatever wisdom we have gained on to others. We accepted others for what they are, seeing them as growing like we are and part of humankind's diversity. Our sense of community continually expands as we prepare for survival of the spirit beyond our mortality.

THE POINT

Developing through each subsequent stage of life grants us greater control over our happiness and well-being.

In Sunrise Stage, a person is wholly dependent on other people's actions and approval to be happy. This is a horrible strategy because other people are unpredictable and unreliable.

In Sunshine Stage, one becomes reliant on oneself, but they're still reliant on external success to be happy — making money, accolades, victory, conquests, etc. These are more controllable than other people, but they are still mostly unpredictable in the long-run.

Sunset Stage relies on a handful of relationships and endeavours that proved themselves resilient and worthwhile through Stage Two. These are more reliable. This Stage requires we only hold on to what we've already accomplished as long as possible.

At each subsequent stage, happiness becomes based more on internal, controllable values and less on the externalities of the ever-changing outside world.

INTER-STAGE CONFLICT

Later stages don't replace previous stages. They transcend them. Sunshine Stage people still care about social approval. They just care about *something more* than social approval. In Sunset Stage people still care about testing their limits. They just care more about the commitments they've made.

Each stage represents a reshuffling of one's life priorities. It's for this reason that when one transitions from one stage to another, one will often experience fallout in one's friendships and relationships. If you were Sunshine Stage and all of your friends were Sunshine Stage, and suddenly you settle down, commit and get to work on Sunset Stage, yet your friends are still in Sunshine Stage, there will be a fundamental disconnect between your values and theirs that will be difficult to overcome.

WHAT GETS US STUCK

The same thing gets us stuck at every stage: a sense of personal inadequacy.

People get stuck at Sunrise Stage because they always feel as though they are somehow flawed and different from others, so they put all of their effort into conforming into what those around them would like to see. No matter how much they do, they feel as though it is never enough.

In Sunshine Stage people get stuck because they feel as though they should always be doing more, doing something better, doing something new and exciting, improving at something. But no matter how much they do, they feel as though it is never enough.

At Sunset Stage people get stuck because they feel as though they have not generated enough meaningful influence in the world, that they make a greater impact in the specific areas that they have committed themselves to. But no matter how much they do, they feel as though it is never enough.

One could even argue that at the last Stage, people feel stuck because they feel insecure that their legacy will not last or make any significant impact on the future generations. They cling to it and hold onto it and promote it with every last gasping breath. But they never feel as though it is enough.

MORE ON STAGES OF LIFE

Significant changes in human life occurred in a seven years segment or there about.

Here are seven years segmentations of human life from cradle to after retirement.

PERIOD	YEARS	STAGES EFFECT
	1	
	2	
	3	Period of Infancy
	4	
	5	
	6	
	7	

	8	
	9	Period of
	10	Childhood
	11	
	12	Beginning of
	13	Individual Responsibility
	14	
	15	
	16	Period of
YOUTH PERIOD.	17	Adolescence
ALL	18	
JUVENILE	19	
GRACES	20	
ADORNED	21	
	22	
	23	Period of

	24	Attainment of
	25	Full Growth.
	26	
	27	
	28	
YOUNG MAN OR	29	
WOMAN IN FULL	30	Period of
DEVELOPMENT OF	31	Construction.
VITAL STRENGTH	32	Person Acquire
AND EQUILIBRIUM	33	Property, Possessions,
	34	A Home and Family.
	35	
STILL ON THE	36	Period of Reactions & Changes.
UPGRADE TOWARDS	37	Effort Made in All Preceding Years
THE DAZZLING	38	Been Maintained By The Prospect
HEIGHTS OF	39	Of The Vast Horizons To Be Dominated.
MATURITY.	40	Road Traversed Is Contemplated With
	41	Pride, But With Emotion.

SUMMIT REACHED.   42   Turn Towards The Abyss Whose Dizzy

43   Curves Wind Steeply Into

44   Ever-Increasing Darkness.

45

46   Period of Reconstruction,

47   Adjustment And Recuperation.

48   Getting Ready For Next

49   Seven Years Cycle.

PLANNING TOWARDS 50   Halfway Down The Slope.

RETIREMENT FROM 51   Path Of Life Still Illuminated

PHYSICAL WORKS. 52   By The Light From The Peaks,

MUST STARTS 53   Though Already touched By The

HERE.   54   Chill Of The Abyss.

55   Organ Weakened And Compelled

56   To Submit To Numerous Abdications.

57

58

59   Entrance of The Cold Melancholy

60   Valleys.

61   Resigned To Inexorable Destiny.

62   Stand On The Threshold Of Old Age.

63

64

65   Begin Preparations For The Long

66   Journey That Must Inevitably Be

67   Undertaken.

68

69

70

71   Wrinkled And Old,

72   Endowed With Numerous

73   Infirmities.

74   Sits In The Waiting Room For

75   The Last Journey.

76   Consider It A Miracle That

77   You Are Still Alive.

78

79

80

81   At Over Eighty; Amazing

82   Phenomenon.

83   You Are Treated With The Respect

84   Due To Antiquities.

EVERYTING THAT LIVES HAS PERIODS OF BIRTH, OF GROWTH AND FRUITAGE AND OF DEATH.

FOUR GRAND QUARTERS OF LIFE.

Life means to live and Age is a prejudice. The fact that a year represents one complete revolution of the earth round the sun has nothing in common with the evolution of the human being . To be so many years old means simply that the circling seasons have been observed so many times and nothing more. It implies no consideration of the intelligent of the person or his physical state. A forty years old man may be younger in the real meaning of the word than a man of twenty. Nevertheless there are some common phenomenon.

At twenty years, you see a youth or a young girl adorned with all the juvenile graces.

At thirty years, a young man or woman is in the full development of vital strength and equilibrium, still on the upgrade towards the dazzling heights of maturity.

At forty years, the summit has been reached, the effort made having been maintained by the prospect of the vast horizons to be dominated.

At fifty years, you are halfway down the slope, which is still illumined by the light from the peaks, though already touched by the chill of the abyss, an organism weakened and compelled to submit to numerous renunciations.

At sixty years you proceed to the cold melancholy valleys. You accept destiny and stand on the threshold of old age. You begin to prepare for the long journey that must inevitably be undertaken.

At seventy years, wrinkled and old, endowed with numerous infirmities, you sit in the waiting room for the last journey home.

By your eightieth year, it becomes an amazing phenomenon and you are treated with the respect due to antiquities.

Let us consider the division of the life span into four grand quarters represented by Spring, Summer, Autumn and Winter.

The Spring stands for infancy, childhood and youth, the irresponsible and educational period from the first to the twenty-first year of life. This is when one is fitted by service and study for the next important stage, It is the time when fidelity and offspring reverence, obedience are instilled into the growing mind.

The Summer quarter of life from twenty-one to forty-two is the practical period of life, and is concerned with the life of the householder, in which wealth becomes an object, responsibility grows, and the duties of life becomes heavier and filled with business activity. It is the period when the social side of the personality is expressed and the lesson of unselfishness is learned. Prosperity comes with the fullness of life which abounds in the summer portion. The virtues developed are caution, thrift, charity, magnanimity, diligence and prudence. Charles Haanel in his book 'Master Key System' explained that this period is governed by the sign Leo, in which the life forces bum at their greatest heat and love for partner and offspring finds its greatest height in the domestic and social world.

The Autumn quarter of life is one in which the glory of manhood and the fullness of motherhood are turned to wider interest and personal claims are sacrificed for the benefit of those outside the narrow circle of the home. The national welfare are taken up with motives that are less limited and more altruistic in their nature, the desire being to help in the ruling and guiding of those who belong to the nation. The virtues to be acquired are equilibrium, justice, strength, courage, vigour and generosity. Charles Haanel explained this period to be denoted by the sign Scorpio, symbol of self-controlled emotions, fixed feelings and permanent modes of action

The Winter stage of life is the period in which experience is garnered and the lessons of life are stored ready for the enriching of the ego. It is the stage in which the review of life brings wisdom and the tender feelings of sympathy to all. The virtues of the last three signs are made manifest as patience, self-sacrifice, service, purity, wisdom, gentleness and compassion. Aquarius sign centralise the mind and brings the climax when the man is complete and the humanized perfection of manhood culminates in the one whose mind is wholly centred in higher states of consciousness.

This is the normal nature's plan for humanity. To what degree of conformity an individual is to this nature's plan is a different thing entirely.

CHAPTER SIX

WHY?

What ultimately is career and life success? What are we striving for? Why? What is our reason to be? The answer to these questions, and the significance we find in each of the life stages, will be very different depending on which world view we take.

There are two worldviews, Naturalism and Supernaturalism. Naturalism is based on the assumption that human reason is supreme and this world (*i.e.* nature) is all there is. Supernaturalism is based on the assumption that there is more - that beyond nature as we know it there is an intelligence far surpassing our puny human intellects and we are charting our courses to a higher place.

If Naturalism is our world-view, much of this life, including the life stages, doesn't make much sense. There is no ultimate goal. We perfect ourselves more every step of the way in life and then, at the height of our growth, we cease to exist. Not a very motivating scenario. Also a risky scenario. If we were betting on the wrong world view the negative consequences are far more severe and lasting than anything that happens to us in this life.

Naturalism's idea that we humans represent the ultimate intelligence can seem - at least momentarily - very sophisticated and flattering to our egos. Many very intelligent people have been seduced by this idea and spent their entire lives stuck in this rut. However, inevitably, those who have tried to replace God with human reason (especially when it has been their own reason they decided to revere) have done more harm than good. They have usually also ended up disillusioned and unhappy. However well-meaning their original intentions were, the seduction of power - the idea of 'being' rather than 'serving' God - got them, and us, in trouble.

The result has been much suffering, pain, unequal justice, and bad things happening to good people in this world. Hitler and Stalin occur to us as two extreme examples of people who took this path. Naturalism has not given us much to celebrate. The reality of Naturalism is that, when we get beyond its original seductions, it tends to keep our gaze focused down, on the mud. Most of us from the depths of our too often neglected souls ache for more. Something in our innermost being cries out for a higher purpose - real meaning and goals that can be more satisfying and enduring than the transient successes, the 'vanities' of this life. We long to make that all-important simple turn of the head. We don't want this troubled existence to be all there is. We want to lift up our eyes beyond the restricted ceiling of earth and hope for heaven.

Supernaturalism gives us that hope. Supernaturalism goes substantively beyond Naturalism and provides meaning, even to our sufferings. Supernaturalism makes life a positive journey towards a higher place, with rewards far surpassing anything Naturalism can promise. Also, not only our spiritual, but even our finest scientific leaders tell us the 'faith' of Supernaturalism is much more consistent with the universe's observed logic and order than Naturalism's faith in the chaos of nothingness built solely on chance. Supernaturalism gives us an over-arching reason to be, an ultimate destination. Fortunately, it turns out that the most advanced modern research on life stages helps outline a path to that destination with defined way stations that can help us map our progress during the journey.

They tell us the purpose of each stage is to further our growth - to increase our learning and give us new, more mature insights. Our primary purpose in life is not business, money, recognition, professional expertise or career progression. Our primary purpose is to become complete human beings and to help others become complete human beings as we work together in cooperative community on resolving the issues of each life stage. How open we stay to this never-ending learning and how effectively we assimilate and grow from the often painful insight of each stage, seem to be critical determining factors in how far we progress - and in whether or not we experience satisfaction and the peace that can only come from movement towards an ultimately meaningful goal.

Effective progression through the stages is congruent with what generations of spiritual writers have defined as the real purpose of life, spiritual growth - the process of purifying and preparing ourselves for a higher life. This is much more important than what specific career field or profession we choose, or how much material recognition and reward we receive for what we do. A successful career is one that enhances our spiritual growth. Our occupational choice should be one that can best enhance that growth. In later chapters we will present some proven techniques for helping us make that important choice.

If you continually track your progress, as we recommend, you may find you even want to change career fields occasionally as you progress over the years, reach plateaus, and need new challenges to start you towards the next stage.

There are many who have received very high levels of material recognition and reward, but appear to be frozen and unhappily stagnated at one of the lower level life stage way stations. Likewise there are people who are wise and at peace in very high level developmental stages who have never sought or received much material recognition and reward. Which group would you consider more successful?

There is nothing wrong with material success and recognition, if they don't distract us from more enduring realities and endeavours. If material success and recognition become ends in themselves, if they define the ultimate destination in our career and life journeys - there has been a great deal of social, psychological and spiritual wisdom accumulated over the centuries - that tells us we will find arrival at that ultimate destination terribly disappointing.

The rich man in the parables, who ignored the beggar Lazarus at his gate, discovered too late that Lazarus and not he found his final destination in heaven. In recent times we've all read about case after case of wealthy, renowned media, literary and financial personalities who ended their days in very public alcohol or drug ridden despair. Like the poet we cited earlier, most of these probably needed to lift their eyes and discover a higher reality.

We do not, of course, move in simple linear fashion from one stage to another with no going back. It is not that simple. Instead we move through the stages in cyclical fashion, hopeful with a longer term forward momentum, but inevitably cycling back and re-working concerns of earlier stages as we face unpredicted events, traumas and fluctuating career, family or interpersonal situations.

CHAPTER SEVEN

The Financial Planning For Over 50

We all have dreams; we all have aspirations, goals, and desires, in all we all desire to have happiness and harmony particularly at retirement.

The fact is; we can only be happy as long as we are NOT short of the three things which all mankind desires and which are necessary for his highest expression and complete happiness. They are **Good Health**, being in the mist of good friends and family which we call **Love** and most important NOT short of sufficient supply which we call **Wealth**. – Sufficient supply not only to take care of our necessities but also to provide for those comforts and luxuries to which we are entitled and had been accustomed to. The word sufficient may not be absolute as what would be considered sufficient for one would be considered absolute and painful lack for another. At any rate, those who possess all three; Health, Wealth and Love, find nothing else which can be added to their cup of happiness. **Remember that success in its highest and most noble form calls for <u>PEACE OF MIND</u> and <u>ENJOYMENT</u> and <u>HAPINESS</u>. All come to the man who have found all the three above.**

It is therefore very important for us to put in place that mechanism that will give the sufficient supply needed for growing up gracefully and harmoniously. That mechanism is Financial Planning.

For only then may desire be satisfied, harmony attained and happiness secured.

The main goal of financial planning is to be financially independent.

It means the ability to manage your money in such a way that you have sufficient funds to live your chosen lifestyle without assistance from others.

It is having enough money to meet all your needs for the rest of your life whether you are at work or had stopped work.

Our prayer had always been that our later years should be more prosperous than the former. How far had we achieved this?

Dreams are real and we all dream dreams. Between your dream and destiny, there is a roadmap you have to activate or work out to bring the dream to reality and manifestation.

For anybody that is aged 50 and above it is a challenge he/she have to face for the working years will soon run out and to avoid being in a mess you have to examine the true you and determine if financial independence lie within you or not. Even the Scripture says "when are you going to be wise oh fools".

Anybody that is over age 50 is in the evening stage of life span called "The Sunset Age".

We need to take responsibility and organise our life so that our Sunset Age is better than the previous two or else we will join the ranks of those who are coasting their way to retirement.

We need to make our latter years count and be significant such that we will experience a life of purpose and see the fulfilment of our life's mission. As we make progress on the success journey, we will frequently find ourselves standing at crossroads when we will have to make decisions. The decision that we make will either determine the happiness or otherwise.

At this stage I will employ us to put in place a realistic system for achieving true financial independence. I need to inform you that this system have rules. These rules are like money maps for a clear route to your goal of financial independence. Six out of 10 of us never calculate how much will be needed when retired. This figure is like a destination on a map, giving you direction as you save, invest and create your financial plan.

For the person that determined to be financially independent; he/she must develop a plan based on these rules and road signs and put that plan into action. Putting the plan into action is an absolute critical step on the road to <u>wealth, freedom and real peace of mind</u>.

It had been estimated that fully 95% of the people in the Western World DO NOT achieve financial independence by the time of their retirement at age 65 now 70, but rather they end up DEPENDENT on the government, or charity or their family or they have to keep working until they die. Only 5% do not fall into this category.

A lot of us went through our lives believing the myth that if we were just good employees and good consumers, we would be rewarded in the end. Instead, most of us end up struggling to survive on social security or on pitiful small pension. We then end up in TENSION. Tension in the dictionary means the action of stretching something tight, but my own definition is that tension is TEN SIONs – that is SIONs in ten places i.e. CONFUSION, DISTRUPTION, EXHAUSTION, EXTHORTION, DIFFUSION, RADIATION, EVAPORATION, POLLUTION, FRUSTRATION, CORRECTION and all the sions that is stressful to the mind.

FINANCIAL DIFFCULTIES and LACK of LOVE head the list of causes of MIND DISTURBANCES.

 WE SHOULD NOT BE LIKE THE CIRCUS ELEPHANT WHO COULD HAVE EASILY BREAK FREE OF THE SMALL CHAIN TIEING IT DOWN.

It is therefore important to put in place plan that will compel us to break free from the anxiety of financial failure and achieve peace of mind. Peace of mind comes from knowing that we have enough, or will have enough, to provide for ourselves and be financially independent.

You have to put in place a sound, structured plan for achieving your financial goals. Action less is

FAILURE. Failure is the only thing you do not have to work upon to achieve.

PATH TO SUCCESS; is the act of distributing your income systematically so that a definite percentage of it will steadily ACCUMULATE and REINVESTED to bring in additional income. THIS IS THE DEFINITE WAY TO INCREASE WEALTH.

There are four basic ways to get money;

1. **<u>Become an Employee</u>**; - You work for somebody or an organisation and only paid from the profit made by that organisation i.e. your employer. You are only paid to live and come back to work next day. If an employee is financially independent; you need to go and audit his book at the place of work. As you are uplifted in responsibility and wages so goes up your expenses and outgoings.

2. **<u>Becomes a Professional</u>**, a Star, An Artist etc. including inheritance.– Money will come in large number until when peak of

profession is reached and then comes the downward slope of income. If a large sum of money is not put into investment before this downward slope the person will end up a puppet.

3. **Become an Entrepreneur** – This is the first step towards becoming financially independence. In so far as the entrepreneur can put in place a process for which the public is ready to part with their hard earned money for his product or service, he/she will become financially independent particularly if he/she can invest the surplus funds.

4. **Become an Investor** – Here your money works for you. This is financial independence in that your money makes money for you. This should be our target and it involves savings and investing enough so that at some point you have enough money so that the money your money is making will enable you to do whatever you want to do.

The Secrets of Financial Independence.

Save - This is funding your future. How much is enough? This depends on your lifestyle and expenses, potential medical bills and the kind of support you will have from Pension Plan and Social Security. Statistics have shown that a minimum of 10% of your earned income should be put aside for the raining day. The raining day is your retirement period which is bound to come. If you are just over 50, do not despair, since it's not too late to save enough for a comfortable retirement. At 50, you still have 15 years to build up a nest egg if planning to retire at 65, although your savings should begin to gather momentum towards a furious saving.

It also means re-investing your investment's earnings until you are financially independent. The miracle of compounding will also see your investment increase in value as you re-invest the earning from investment. The habit of saving minimum of 10% of income also has the advantage of establishing a pattern of living within your means. Most people get into financial difficulty because of being used to the habit of living beyond their means. Consuming more than produced.

Continuing this practice of consuming less than produced after retirement means that you will never run out of money and resulting growth of your investment helps offset inflation. **BEWARE OF LITTLE EXPENSES THAT PREVENT SAVINGS; A LITTLE LEAK CAN SINK A SHIP.**

Pay Down Your Debt – Pay off all your debits first and only then begin paying yourself. It's the only way to dramatically accelerate your journey to financial independence. When you pay off your debits, you then need less to live on each month because you are only paying for food, utilities, taxes, insurance and any other minor expenses, leaving you with a lot of saveable money each month. For this your retirement investment will build up rapidly because you are funding them at a high level each month. What it means is that you should not mortgage your "LATTER" to pay for your "NOW".

The most devastating debit which should be paid off immediately is your credit cards. It is the most expensive and is sure sign that you are living beyond your means. You can have mortgage on your house (but going into retirement with a large mortgage is not the best situation), credit for education or even taking out a 3 year car loan, if that's the only way you can afford to buy a car, but using credit to finance a vacation or clothing or your groceries means that you are in truth buying something you cannot afford. Trying to be someone you are not and you are not living in integrity with yourself. If you have too many bills, it's because you are spending more than you make. The only solution is to get rid of the credit cards.

If you are loaded down with credit cards debit, the reason you have so much of it is that you are so good at paying back. The reason you have no savings is that you are not good at saving. The only way to break this cycle is to start saving while you pay off the debt.

Put a Retirement Plan in Place – Living within your means does not necessarily mean spending less; that balance could easily be achieved by earning more. You will agree that it is easier to earn extra hundred pounds than to cut a hundred a month in expenses.

Poverty is a state of mind. The lack of money does not cause poverty; it is the poverty mentality that cause or result in a lack of money. That is why giving poor people money could not reduce poverty. If you give a poor person £10,000.00 or £100,000.00 today, in a year's time he is likely to be poor again because their value are based on a poverty mentality so that they spend those money on those things they value; clothes, cars etc. because the basic belief of poor people is that money is to spend. With such believe system, it will be impossible to save or put a retirement plan in place or defer immediate gratification and spend it on things that have a long term pay off like education or obtain a skill for wealth creation. The key to financial independence then is living within your means and saving enough to provide for your future. It is knowing how much is enough and planning towards it.

Invest – Be an Investor and not a Trader. An Investor invests for the long term while the Trader seeks profit by exploiting short-term gains. You have to be a professional to win that game. And while you are at it; do not put all your eggs in one basket.

A well-diversified portfolio means you will always have something going up in value, but it means you will also always have an investment going down. Diversification is the best strategy you have to reduce your risks in volatile financial markets. Your asset allocation should be determined by your stage in the financial life circle, your risk tolerance and your tax situation, and NOT by whatever asset class was hot last year.

Build on Your Successes – The most critical points in your journey to financial independence come at the transition point; when we move from one point to another. When that happens, the best we can do is to build on our past successes, rather than start all over. Look at the strength you have developed and knowledge you have acquired and find new ways to utilise those in a new environment. It is not change that cause the pain; it is the resistance to that changes in our life that causes pain.

In rounding up this roadmap towards becoming financially independent, I would like to say we should not slow down. As Elders even when retired we must not be tired but should re-fire. We need to plan because failure to plan is planning to fail.

There can be no failure for the man who still fight on.

Carrying a burdensome cross temporarily is not FAILURE. If you have the real seed of success within you, a little adversity and temporary defeat will only serve to nurture that seed and cause it to burst forth into maturity.

Unless a beggar resolutely shakes off and irrevocably turns his back on his begging habit, he will forever remain a beggar. For the more he begs, the more he develops the beggar characteristics of lack of initiative, courage, drive and self-reliance.

Do not simply drift in life; visualize your goal or your destination to be reached and the dangers to be avoided. Then go for it.

DESIRE followed by CONCENTRATION will wrench any secret from nature.

The accumulation of material wealth, whether the aim is that of bare existence or for luxury, consumes most of the time that we put into this earthly struggle, in most cases, we find it difficult to change this materialistic tendency of human nature, we can, at least, change the method of pursuing it by adopting cooperation and organised efforts as the basis of the pursuit. **BY THIS WE WILL NOT SELL OUR SOUL FOR A MESS OF POTTAGE AS A BARGAIN.**

Moses reached 80 before he took up leadership of Israel.

Caleb was 85 when he finally received his inheritance. He never lost sight of his life goal and at 85, he was still striving to see it accomplished.

Winston Churchill at a time of life when most people are winding down he was climbing the highest rung of the political ladder to lead Britain against Nazis.

Benjamin Franklin was 70 years of age when he helped to draw up the Declaration of Independence, and 78 when he secured that independence as a Cosignatory of the Treaty of Versailles, at 84, 2 years before his death, he was sitting on the convention that drafted the American Constitution.

John Wesley went on evangelizing into his eighties, and JC Massee into his nineties.

Gladstone was in No 10 Downing Street at 83.

Being effective at old age will come if you allow it. Old age doesn't automatically bring defeat.

Delay is not Denial – you can start late if you are willing.

Inaction leads to ATROPHY which leads to loss of ambition and self –confidence. Unfortunately, these are the essential qualities needed in life to avoid being carried through life on the wings of UNCERTAINITY.

WISDOM AND UNDERSTANDING: THE LANGUAGE OF SUCCESS.

Get wisdom, but above all, get understanding.

Everybody wants and desires peace, joy and sense of fulfilment, a healthy long life and a little bit of money.

Proverb 3:13-18 tell us that happy is the man that finds wisdom and the man that gets understanding. It further analysed various features associated with wisdom and understanding. Among these are riches and honour, length of days, pleasantness and peace. It says it's more precious than rubies and the gain is more than gold. It concluded by saying 'Happy is every one that retains wisdom and understanding'. All these are the attributes of being successful.

Once you have wisdom and understanding, all your heart desire shall be accomplished.

King Solomon requested Wisdom from God and all his wishes were granted.

Fifteen times in the New Testament, Jesus said; 'Hear and Understand', not only hear but understand what was heard.

In many of Jesus' parables, He would say; 'I need you to hear this but I need you to understand. The word 'To Understand' is very important.

Hearing changes nothing; it is understanding that brings direction and action to our lives. We hear many things at various times, but act on only those things we understand. We need wisdom to see our visions and to identify 'the still small voice of God' and to understand them.

Your mind will always block out that which it does not understand. What it block out may be essential to your breakthrough but you need to understand to act accordingly.

Scot Anderson in his book 'Think like a Billionaire Become a Billionaire' narrated a time he visited France for a Pastors Conference and in every restaurant he visited had to order spaghetti only because the menu were only in French which he did not understand.

After seven days he still continues to eat spaghetti even though he longed for something that came from a cow. On the menu was the opportunity to have all the foods his heart desired, but the problem was language barrier. The waiter told him the entire menu in French, so he was not limited by what he heard but limited by his understanding of what was said.

So also in the menu of life; God wants us to have all our hearts desire. He gave us the opportunity to order the abundance of life, but since we don't have the understanding, we continue to stay right in the exact same position, even though we wish for better.

Suppose Scot Anderson begins to learn French, he would have opened a new world of ordering and would have enjoyed more from the menu. He would have had more satisfaction in France as we would have been more successful while enjoying limitless blessing of God.

We therefore need to understand the language of success and be able to enjoy the abundance already place here on earth by our creator. It is time we begin to learn the language of success so we can begin to order all of our hopes and dreams from the menu of life.

In Luke 5:1-9; Simon not only got wisdom, but he also understood. His understanding could have been fuelled by the fact that he had earlier listened to Jesus Christ and was taught by Him out of his ship. The lesson from Christ could have aroused his believe in Jesus to have re-launched his net into the deep and he caught his abundance. This was a fisherman that had toiled all night and had taken nothing.

Until you learn the language and start to understand it, you will never step out into the abundance of success. Let us start to learn the language, so we can begin to order all of our hopes and dreams from the menu of life.

Seek wisdom and above all gain understanding. Nothing can compare to gaining wisdom and understanding.

CHAPTER EIGHT

CONCLUSION

Your Acre Of Diamond

When a child is born into this world, the child is endowed with certain inborn traits, the result of millions of years of evolutionary changes, through thousands of generations of ancestors. Added to these inborn traits, the child acquires many other qualities, according to the nature of the child's environment and the teaching received during early childhood.

You are the sum total of that which was born in you and that which you have picked up from your experiences, what you have thought and what you have been taught since birth. It is the application of this sum total that will determine your success and non application shall result in life's failure. Faculties of the mind, like the limb of the body, atrophy and wither away if not used.

The most impressive lessons are those learned by the young from the old, through highly coloured or emotionalised method of teaching. Inherited wealth has the disadvantage that it too often leads to inaction and loss of self-confidence. Lack of the necessity for struggle lead to weakness of ambition and will-power, it sets up in a person's mind a state of lethargy that leads to the loss of self-confidence. Hence the recipient of inherited wealth mostly lack the motive and enthusiasm needed to acquire and develop knowledge which brings power that ends in success. The need to struggle becomes unnecessary and desire for a goal in life is lost.

There are two great major urges to action; The urge of necessity or the desire to create. By making it easy for your child, you may be depriving the world of a genius. The mind that is driven by the urge of necessity or out of love to create develops more rapidly than does the mind that is never stimulated to greater action than that which is necessary for existence.

When the chicken is to be hatched from its shell, the chick will pip (peck a hole in its shell) with its weak beak to create the crack that will let it out of the shell. The chick starts hitting it beak against the shell in earnest to unzip itself. While this is going on, the mother chicken would not use its stronger beak to liberate the chick. The chick would not last long if helped for the use of the weak beak activates its life and strengthens its beak for use to pick its food henceforth. Such is human life on our road to success. It is the application of all our skill, both inborn or acquired that we will use as the tools in building our temple of success. It is never a smooth road but **OUT OF RESISTANCE COMES STRENGTH**. Success could be attained, by anyone with reasonable intelligence and a real desire to succeed; by following certain process or procedure.

Success and power are always found together. You cannot be sure of success unless you have power. You cannot have power unless you apply all the sum total of your in born traits and the acquired qualities picked up from experiences, thoughts and what you were taught from birth. The world is there for man to conquer and to rule. But he who wants to rule must first school himself and acquire knowledge. Constructive application of the knowledge acquired will give him the power needed to rule the world. This is the glory endowed him by his creator.

We have two periods of our life; one is gathering, classifying and organising knowledge and the second period during which we are struggling for recognition. We must learn something which shall give us the ability and power to serve mankind. This will be followed by confrontation with the problem of convincing the world that we can serve them.

RENDER CONSTRUCTIVE AND USEFUL SERVICE AND YOU WILL EARN A LIVING, FOR THE WORLD WILL PAY FOR IT.

Happiness, the final object of all human effort, is a state of mind that can be maintained only through the hope of future achievement.

Happiness lies always in the future and never the past. The happy person is the one who dreams of heights of achievement that are yet attained. – The home you intend to own, the money you intend to earn and place in the bank, the trip you intend to take when you can afford it, the position in life you intend to fill when you have prepared yourself and the preparation itself – these are the things that produce happiness. Likewise, these are the materials out of which your main goal is formed; these are the things over which you may become enthusiastic, no matter what your main goal in life may be.

We absorb the material for thought from our surrounding environment. Our environment consists of the books we read, the people with whom we associate, the community in which we live, the nature of the work in which we are engage, the country or nation in which we reside, the clothes we wear, the songs we sing and the religion and intellectual training we receive prior to the age of fourteen years.

The mind feeds upon that which we supply or that which is forced upon it, through our environment. It is therefore important to supply our mind with suitable material out of which to carry on its work of attaining our life goal. Our first step is to create in our own mind an exact, clear and well-rounded out picture of the environment in which we believe we could best attain our definite goal and then concentrate our mind upon this picture until we transform it into reality. This is the first principle to be observed in our plans for the achievement of success, and if we fail or neglect to observe it, you cannot succeed except by chance. Our daily associates constitute one of the most important parts of your environment and may work for our progress or our retrogression according to the nature of such associates. Our associates must therefore be those who are in sympathy with our main goals, whose mental attitude inspire us with enthusiasm, self-confidence, determination and ambition.

Any form of group effort, where two or more people form a cooperative alliance for the purpose of accomplishing a goal, becomes more powerful than mere individual effort.

Plain cooperative effort produces power; there can be no doubt about this, but cooperative effort that is based upon complete harmony of purpose develops superpower.

Men who had been successful have been known as able organisers in that they possessed the ability to enlist the cooperative efforts of other men who supplied talent and ability which they themselves did not possess. The organisation must consist of individuals each of whom supplies some specialized talent which the other members of the organisation do not possess. Success in life cannot be attained except through peaceful, harmonious, cooperative effort. Success cannot be attained single-handed or independently. Fortunes that are acquired through cooperative effort inflict no scars upon the hearts of their owners, but not so for fortunes that are acquired through conflict and competitive methods that border on extortion.

There are three major motivating forces to which man responds in practically all of his efforts;-

1. The motive of self-preservation.
2. The motive of sexual contact
3. The motive of financial and social power.

Nothing is impossible to the person who knows what it is he wants and makes up his mind to acquire it. Opportunities, Capital, Cooperation from other men and all other essentials for success mobilize and gravitate to the man who knows what he wants.

WE DO WELL THAT WHICH WE LOVE TO DO.

Give a man the sort of work that harmonizes with his nature and the best in him will exert itself. One of the outstanding tragedies of the world is the fact that most people never engage in the work for which they are best fitted by nature.

Success in its highest and noblest form calls for peace of mind and enjoyment and happiness which come only to the man who has found the work that he likes best.

To achieve anything in this world, you must rely upon the forces within your own mind for your start. It is after this start has been made that you may turn to others for aid and assistant, but the first step must be taken without outside aid. After you have made this 'start', you will be surprised to observe how many willing people you will encounter who will volunteer to assist you.

Until you know your goal in life, you are nothing but a drifter, subject to control by every stray wind of circumstances that blow in your direction.

The mystery of life is such that we come here without our consent from whence we know not! We go away without our consent, wither, we know not!

Everywhere around us, we have some characters called 'never do well people'. One of their outstanding features is procrastination. Lack of action has caused them to slip backward until they got into a rut situation where they will remain unless by accident, they are forced out into the open road of struggle where unusual action will become necessary.

Unless you develop the habit of expressing yourself in action, you will be doing the goose step down the dusty road of failure.

The common excuse of such is 'The world will not give me a chance'. The world never gives anyone a chance. A man who wants a chance must create it through action. He will meet with disappointment if he waits for someone to hand it to him on a silver platter. Inaction is the commonest causes of poverty and of failure.

Go to the ant, thou sluggard; consider her ways, and be wise: Which having no guide, overseer or ruler, provide her meat in the summer, and gathered her food in the harvest. How long will thou sleep, O sluggard? When will thou arise out of your sleep? Yet a little, a little slumber, a little folding of the hands to sleep; so shall thy poverty come as one that travel and your want as an armed man.

It had been said earlier that self-impoverishment is where an individual decides not to pursue means of wealth creation. Ability to create is the catalyst to success. Every person created has been endowed with some potential talents or skills. No one is born blank. It your ability to apply those skills and talents in the form of service for mankind such that the remuneration that follows will be able to take you out of poverty line.

See thou a man diligent in his business? He shall stand before kings; he shall not stand before mean men.

It is he who has no definite focus, goal or ambition in life that falls into the category of a sluggard as above and a failure. No individual is created to be a failure since anybody with average intelligent, by following some procedure, will end up being a success. It is a choice, desire and determination followed by the right attitude.

Remember it had been said earlier that success in its highest and most noble form calls for PEACE OF MIND and ENJOYMENT and HAPINESS; but not material wealth or big fat bank account. It is therefore imperative to conclude with some tips that can enhance such success up till retirement and beyond;

1. Your work is the thing that you do to contribute your skills, experience, labour or knowledge to society in some way. It is also a way for you to "self-actualize" and create positive stress in your life. Even when you leave the traditional workplace, you will still have a need to share your workplace strengths

116

and transferable skills. If you have a positive attitude towards the workplace, then the desire to have a retirement free from any kind of work becomes irrelevant. A wise person once said, "If you love what you do, you never have to work again!" By the way, work doesn't have to be full-time, it doesn't have to be something you don't like to do, and it doesn't even have to be for pay! Many retirees use volunteering as a way to replace the things that they miss most about their previous work.

2. Our close personal relationships define us, give us a purpose for living our lives and encourage us to create life goals. We all have a basic need to share our lives, experiences and life journey with those closest to us in retirement our friendships and close relationships may offer us the validation that we may have received in the workplace. Those relationships give us the opportunity to "connect" on many levels with someone close and to share ourselves. Psychologists have identified our desire to share ourselves as a basic human need. This need is often satisfied in the activities that we enjoy with our spouse or partner, friends and family. Researchers have found that people in satisfying personal relationships have fewer illnesses and higher levels of good overall health. That's the clinical rationale. In

real life terms, having people close to you who will share your life and be there for you will not only add to your overall life enjoyment, but will also add years on to your life!

3. As you get older, your social support network becomes increasingly important. You draw your social support network from a much broader social network. Successful retirees generally have robust social networks that provide them with friendship, fulfilling activities and life structure. As part of your retirement plan, you might want to think about the quality of the social network that you have today and your plans to build it. One of the lessons that we can learn about the aging process is that our social networks begin to shrink–if we aren't continually adding to them. You can join clubs, meet new people and get out of the house to do new things. In retirement you are going to want a lot of people who you can count on and it makes good sense to continue to seek out new opportunities to socialize.

4. Leisure is a fundamental human need. We use it to recharge our batteries, to act as a diversion in our

lives, to create excitement, anticipation or simply to rest and contemplate. Things change, however, when leisure becomes the central focus of our lives. Leisure, by its very nature, loses its lustre when it is the norm in our life rather than the diversion. For many retirees, the idea of leisure is associated with "not having to do anything". In the end, a lack of stimulation affects our mental and emotional state and then ultimately our physical well-being. There is a big difference between "time-filling" activities and "fulfilling" activities that we look forward to. In retirement, leisure activities often replace workplace functions to meet the basic needs that we have. Successful retirees balance their leisure over many different activities and take the opportunity to do new things and not get into a rut.

5. Some retirees feel that a happy retirement is guaranteed by financial security. However, there is no price tag on successful retirement. As someone once said, "having a million pound is NOT a retirement plan!" Financial comfort refers to being able to manage your life in a satisfying and fulfilling way using the financial resources that you have. If financial discomfort contributes to retirement stress, then your financial plan becomes a negative rather than a positive. The keys to achieving financial

comfort are to have a clear understanding of the financial resources you have and the demands on your money that will come from the life you lead (both now and in the future). One good way to look at your financial situation in this next life phase is to think about the three "buckets" that you will have to keep filled in order to achieve financial comfort:

- Your "essentials" bucket, which will pay for all of your basic needs
- Your "lifestyle" bucket, which will fund those fun things that you dream of doing in retirement
- Your "nest egg" bucket, which will fund any emergencies that may arise, provide you with a sense of security through good and challenging times and ultimately will form part of your legacy.

Do have a successful life.

TO GOD IS THE GLORY.